Guru Meditation

Songs & Stories

Guru Meditation

David Gullen & Gaie Sebold

Copyright © David Gullen & Gaie Sebold 2024
All rights reserved

ISBN-13: 9798875915970

The right of the authors to be identified as the authors of this work has been asserted in accordance with the Copyright, Designs and Patents Act 1988.

All rights reserved. No part of this publication may be reproduced or stored in a retrieval system, or transmitted in any form or by any means without the written consent of the copyright holders.

No part of this publication may be used in any way to train, inform, or provide source learning data for any Large Language Model based chatbot or any other type of artificial neural network without the written consent of the copyright holders.

Bluebell Apocalypse first published in BSFA Fusion #2, Vol 2, 2022
And into the Tunnel, the Train first published in BFS Horizons #16, 2023

Cover design by David Gullen
Interior layout by David Gullen

A Nellug/D'Lobes Production

For the NHS

Contents

Introduction 1

Songs

We Love Life Whenever We Can 5
The Seven Stages of Living With Cancer 6
Carpe Diem 9
Go Gently 10
Tolerating the Insult 11
It Ain't Necessarily So 14
Guru Meditation Error 15
Tick 18
Parkrun 19
Solstice 20

Stories

Bluebell Apocalypse 25
And into the Tunnel, the Train 35
Autumn 43

About Prostate Cancer 55
Acknowledgements 56
About the Authors 59

Introduction

As writers, we are prone to – some would say born to – document our ideas, thoughts, opinions and experiences. Whatever life throws at us. We suffer and we rejoice the same as everybody else but we also pin the details of those experiences. I was reminded of a pithy line from Adrian Mitchell's dystopian poem "On the Beach at Cambridge" (1984): "You're a poet, said the Regional Commissioner, Go out and describe that lot." I was also reminded, as ever, of Emily Dickinson's famous dictum: "Tell all the truth but tell it slant."

In this vital and timely book, my friend David Gullen, supported by his loving wife Gaie Sebold, bravely addresses the diagnosis, progression, suffering and often excruciating treatment procedures relating to his battle with prostate cancer. Sometimes he faces the insidious demon head-on in a powerfully honest piece such as "The Seven Stages of Living With Cancer". On other occasions, Dave's and Gaie's response is more slant – parodying Gilbert and Sullivan lyrics, or in the short stories that show us how fragile and random is our hold on life. These are despatches from the trenches as David Gullen finds solace and power in gardening, in writing, in small step achievements, in family – "my three kids, and yes, they're grown but... You want to see their kids too." Underpinning all of this is a renewed celebration of "All the things that make life what it is" and an acceptance that death when it comes is a natural conclusion to life, echoing the famous verses from the "Book of Ecclesiastes". Maybe the Ancients had it right – Carpe diem and "To everything there is a season."

Ultimately, this is an emotionally enriching and inspiring tale of survival. Great to still have you with us, Dave.

Allen Ashley, British Fantasy Award Winner,
London. June 2024

Songs

We Love Life Whenever We Can

Because life is magic and no one knows
How that bold flower grows in this stone wall
Or what wind-blown journey each seed has made.

We should love life like a borrowed thing.
Look after it. Let it look after you.
Learn to use it in the best ways you can.
Until the day you must give it back.

D.G.

The Seven Stages of Living With Cancer

In her 1969 book "On Death and Dying" the psychiatrist Elizabeth Kübler Ross wrote that grief could be divided into five stages. Later, a 7-stage model aimed to express the complexities of grief more effectively.

Neither model will necessarily reflect your own experience. You may find it useful to write down your own set of stages as a way to understanding your own emotions.

1. Shock
2. Grief
3. Anger
4. Depression
5. Anger
6. Blame
7. Anger
8. Self-pity
9. Anger
10. Bitterness
11. Anger
12. Regret
13. Anger
14. Acceptance
15. Anger
16. Determination
17. Anger
18. Planning
19. Anger
20. Fatigue
21. Undirected Fury
22. Anger
23. A Sense of Existential Persecution
24. Anger
25. Directed Fury

26. Anger
27. Fatigue
28. Anger
29. Re-Acceptance
30. Anger
31. Travel
32. Anger
33. More Grief
34. Anger
35. Tranquility
36. Anger
37. Incandescent Rage
38. Laughter
39. Anger
40. A Burning Sense of Injustice
41. Anger
42. Fatigue
43. Anger
44. Again, Grief
45. Anger
46. Hope
47. Anger
48. Positive Creativity
49. Anger
50. Introspection
51. Anger
52. Fatigue
53. Anger
54. Further Acceptance
55. Anger
56. Enjoyment of a Normal Day
57. Anger
58. Fatigue
59. Anger
60. An all-encompassing Understanding of how Your Entire Life has brought you to a moment of astonishing Insight; Death is The Inevitable Codicil to Life, and All Will be Well.
61. Anger
62. A return to Hope

63. Anger
64. Trying New Things
65. Anger
66. Gardening
67. Actually, I feel OK right Now
68. Anger
69. Gardening
70. Anger
71. Anger While Gardening
72. Fatigue
73. Anger
74. More Grief
75. Anger
76. Think of a Number Between 1 and 75.

Carpe Diem

When each good day seems as fragile as an egg
How hard it is to simply hold its shape.
Too desperate a grip will shatter it.

G.S.

Go Gently

Imagine how peaceful it will be to lie in the dark,
Resting in silence and surrounded by silence,
and feel your memories decline.

Of what was done
or not done or should have been done,
and was not. All our wants and needs,
all hurt, all wounds, all gone.
Feel what made you cry alone at night
fade away and, like you, decay.

The things that bite and gnaw,
feel them fade, all fade away.

no dreams
no pain
no memory
no breath
no doubt
no lust
no guilt
no love
no broken heart
no struggle
no striving
no failure
no triumph
no tears
can reach you here.

D.G.

Tolerating the Insult*

I take the very model of a modern pharmaceutical
While side effects detach my fingernails from my cuticles.
I'm acquainted with phlebotomy and venous intubay-ti-on
Enduring many broken nights for frequent micturay-ti-on.
They give me gadolinium to clarify my MRI
And radioactive antimatter - dammit I still cannot fly,
A shame I get no superpowers it might make up for some of this
The canula gets so much use my arms are coloured amethyst.

I dodge the common cold as well as viruses pandemical
While tolerating insults psychological and chemical.
In short, in all things steroid, neutropenic and androgenal
I take the very model of a modern pharmaceutical.

Docetaxel beat me up, I noted in my journical
Furosemide prevents my legs from turning pachydermical.
Goserelin's a splendid luteinising hormone agonist
But shriveled up my nutssack that once was so very hard to miss.
There's Cyclazine and Dexamethasone to keep sickness at bay

Lansoprazole's a protein pump inhibitor or so they say
I've no idea what that means but it stops my guts eating themselves
Filgrastim (wasn't he a dwarf in Tolkien?) boosts my white blood cells.

The sheer amount of pills I take seems somewhat disproportionate
Yet half are to control the other drugs' effects unfortunate
In short, in all things steroid, neutropenic and androgenal
I take the very model of a modern pharmaceutical.

I strive to be a model patient for the weary NHS
The while my arse is hanging out the rear end of a backless dress,
Use weights to build my muscles using methods now canonical
And strengthen all my bony parts with acid alendronical.
I'm very good at keeping all my records and my symptoms logged
I note them in a spreadsheet for the days my hippocampus fogs.
I learned the names of every single nurse upon the chemo ward
The cakes I bake them aren't enough and yet they're a sincere reward.

And though I get fed up of it I'm very glad that they are here
To give me lotions potions pills injections scans and mental cheer
So bring on all things steroid, neutropenic and androgenal
Let's have the very model of a modern pharmaceutical.

G.S. & D.G.

*One of Dave's doctors talked about how well, or not, his body tolerated the insult of chemotherapy. Somehow the mad list of drugs and treatments and side-effects became a pastiche of Gilbert & Sullivan's song, The Modern Major General, from The Pirates of Penzance.

It Ain't Necessarily So

Being given an appointment
You've been told you have to keep.
Does not fucking help.
You plod towards it unthinking, like a sheep.

I might get knocked down by the S4 bus,
An eagle might drop a tortoise on my head*
And I'd still be dead.

D.G.

*In 455 BC the renowned Greek playwright, Aeschylus, who fought Persian invaders at Marathon, Salamis, and Plataea, was killed this way.

Guru Meditation Error

You tell me I'm on a Journey.
Like what, some trip to Japan?
Or your daily commute
to work for the Man?

You say I'm on a Journey
like I'm going to learn something,
like my consciousness will expand.
Ooh! Nirvanha. Zen.

You think I'll come back and show you my Instagram?
Where I bought my kaftan in Katmandu?
Let me share some highlights with you.

Here's the blue rug where I passed out and fell;
Nights spent soaking wet, hotter than hell.
My legs thickened and swelled like trunks of trees.
Was life in a wheelchair the new life for me?
On hands and feet, all my nails one by one,
loosened and fell, toes, fingers and thumbs.
What quiet horror. What disgust and shame.
I hated my body worse than the pain.

Would you sit beside me on my bed
when I wept with frustration and fear

and I could not, could not, could not stop?
My wife did.

Shared experience.
That's what this journey's about.
Hahahahaha.

And yet...
Here's the dawn we watched the sunrise,
and I thought that is beautiful.
She took my hand in hers and said
'Loves ya,' and I said, 'Loves ya back.'
These days we laugh so much.

I don't know what I feel but I know one thing: I wish I wasn't here.
Someone tied a label to my coat,
I'm an emigrant, my right to remain revoked,
while so many people try to keep me afloat.

Was there a time I was standing on the platform
waiting for this train? Because I can't remember.
One moment it was just another day, the next I'm in sudden, unexpected danger,
In a room full of strangers.
One of them tells me where I'm going but not how long the ride might be.
Well, I didn't know and nobody there could tell me.

And I still didn't know, and what I thought then, what
I'm still think now is my darling wife, and will I see
another spring, and how will she do the things we do
together, alone?
And my three kids, and yes, they're grown
But you want to see it all, don't you?
You want to see their kids too.
All the things that make life what it is. Life. Life worth
living, worth doing, worth hanging around for.
And I'm walking, not really walking, trying so damned
hard to walk a few steps through the cold sunshine in
green dappled woods along an earthy track.
Still wondering 'How many more springs?'
So much effort to move two steps forwards, three steps
back.

You tell me I'm on a Journey
Like all your tickets are returns.
When you feel the avalanche slide
I hope you'll avoid my personal ride,
but understand this, time and tide,
ride one you will, no chance to choose.
What now seems hypothetical
Is no longer theoretical
When it becomes your personal news.

D.G.

Tick

A clock ticks in my head. It has no hands.
It tells me nothing but that time goes by.
I hate it. Hate its blank and stupid face,
its dumb relentless tick, and tick, and tick.

It taps like bony fingers on my skull
and never stops. I hear it all the time.
Through conversation. Laughter. Through the sound
of spade in earth, through birdsong, everything.

I hear it when you speak, I hear it when
I wake at night and listen to you breathe,
and through the passing of a single car
on some lone nightbound journey. Tick, and tick.

I hate its meaningless and empty sound
I hate its stain on every simple joy
I hate its endless measuring of loss…
But how I dread the moment that it stops.

G.S.

Parkrun

Parkrun, Parkrun has been such fun
Can't run? Just Walk. Parkstroll, Parktalk
That's how it began
For me.

5K Your Way that first slow day
Leant me power for that long hour
I made it round
Thank you.

I was so slow, I was so big
Now I'm less slow, a rolling rig
My wheels fell off, Now they're back on
Thanks in large part to that Parkrun

D.G.

There is very good evidence exercise is the most excellent medicine for both physical and mental health. It has worked well for me.

Solstice

Match box, paper and pen.
Five bulbs, a pot, good earth.

The things we will leave behind,
Write them down.
Burn them in the winter dark,
So they are gone.

We will carry only good things tomorrow
A glad heart, adventure, a coming child.
Write them down.
Plant them with the winter bulbs,
And watch them grow.

D.G.

Stories

Introduction

I wrote my two stories here between one and two years after diagnosis, still trying to come to terms with the seismic shifts in my life. With much of my writing being science fiction and fantasy instinctively I wrote in that genre.

Oblique to my situation these tales may be, but I was pleased with them. The first captured my feelings of having the ground cut away from under my feet, the second the sense of being diminished, of having so much of your life stripped away from you. They also are about, because I needed them to be and because it is true, love and hope.

One quickly found a home in a magazine, and the other won a competition, so I was pleased with them that way too.

The third story, *Autumn*, is written by Gaie and is all kinds of beautiful.

In recent years I have found wisdom and good advice everywhere. We all have a voice, we all deserve to be heard.

David

Bluebell Apocalypse

AT FIRST we didn't take it seriously. I mean, who doesn't like bluebells, and anyway, Nature, right? The surreal truth that overnight, though not even overnight, just blink or look away and there they were, was elided by our amazement and our delight. How did that happen? True sensawunda.

Bluebells everywhere, where they should be and where they shouldn't. Alongside the highways, which was lovely, (who doesn't like bluebells), in the woods and our gardens, ditto. But across the fairways and soccer pitches was a bit much, and the highways and other roads themselves. Bluebells pushed up through the tarmac of the highways and broke through the concrete paths, brimming in what had only a moment ago been fields of corn. Masie and I wondered if this was some incredible nature rebellion protest group. What synchronisation, what resources. For a few brief days bluebells frothed across the Sahara, smothered the Australian outback, the great plains of North America, the Amazon and the Siberian steppe. Somebody actually bothered to look and yes, we really did have a truly blue moon. And Mars. What was going on beneath the scalding acid clouds of Venus was impossible to say, but it seemed a reasonable assumption. The sun?

And every field of crops we once had. Yes, we had a problem.

In those early days I didn't go to work, the trains didn't run, the pavements were too dangerous, cars and busses drifted and slid on a mush of crushed bluebell juice more slippery than ice.

Masie borrowed my golf shoes, wore three extra pairs of socks and walked to the hospital. I suggested she take the garden spade and that turned out to be a very good call. Fourteen hours later she was back home, exhausted and hungry.

'People are dying, John. We can't get to them.'

The lights flickered and steadied again. There had been half a dozen brown-outs in the street through the day and one five minute outage. We had solar on the roof and thank God the bluebells didn't grow there, only on the ground.

'And thank God the hospital has its own generators,' Masie said.

Should we, I wondered, actually be thanking God?

Those were difficult days but we made it through. It was easier for us than many others and at least we made it. Once again the skies were clear of aeroplanes, but this time it had not been a slow decline and recovery. Airliners are not designed to land on fields of bluebells where the runways used to be. There were over ten thousand jets in the air when every landing strip effectively disappeared. A million people. Some few made it down safely. And the rest came down anyway. It doesn't bear thinking about. Everyone knew someone.

Then a moment came, blink or look away and they were gone. No more bluebells, none at all, not even where they were supposed to grow, or anywhere they had grown before.

The damage was done, with infrastructure wrecked, bare fields, and the whole world wondering what it was going to eat.

And yes, as it turned out, the sun too. Absorption spectra showed, fleetingly, a brief, intense burst of carbon, nitrogen, and oxygen. Who in their right mind would cover the sun in bluebells?

'God must like bluebells,' Masie said that evening.

'Or not.'

'Maybe they were leftovers. You know, giveaways.'

'Then God's not much of a gardener.'

'I suppose you have to try these things to see if they work.'

'Masie, please.'

'I'm sorry, I'm just trying to find something to laugh about in all this.' She pushed herself across the sofa into my arms. 'Anything.'

We thought we'd been smart with the pandemic. We told ourselves we'd seen it coming, bought and stocked a chest freezer, and filled one of the small outbuildings we had with dry and canned goods. When the pandemic was over it had become a habit we'd maintained.

'I like it,' Masie said, 'There's something atavistic about having a full food store, it makes me feel safe.'

I agreed, and I was glad we had it too. Towards the end our meals might get boring, but little suburban preppers that we were, we had vitamin supplies too. We could keep ourselves fed for about three months, stretch it out to four. Now it wasn't going to be enough.

I worried about security as much as anything. The first rule of Food Stash Club? Looking back we knew we should have told nobody, but who had we told, and more to the point, who had *they* told? We never used to, but now we locked up everything at night.

A month beyond the bluebell apocalypse the country was still functioning mostly normally. Everything was rationed, and by everything I mean everything. Milk was a millionaire's luxury. Crops had been replanted across the world and we were being told that while things were difficult, we'd pull on through. It seemed clear to me that for many people this was not going to be true.

'John?' Masie sat on the edge of the bed looking at the blue silk material of what had until very recently been her dressing gown. Nude, she stood in front of the wardrobe holding both doors open. 'John, have you...?'

I hadn't, and clearly neither had she. I thought, perhaps, this was her joke until I opened the chest of drawers and saw what was there. It would have needed to be an excessively elaborate joke.

There was a kind of logic here, in the amount of material available, but apart from that the sheer effort, the level of detail was all kinds of crazy. All my shirts were now trousers, all my socks and underwear were trousers too. Tiny little ones. Had I in some moment blinked and looked away, or had I just not noticed that trousers fit for a long-legged and fat-bellied clown now hung each side of the windows? I will never know. Downstairs in the hall a collection of wool and waterproof trousers hung where the coats and scarves used to be, and on the hooks in the kitchen for the tea towels.

'John?'

Masie looked down at me from the top of the stairs. Two pairs of red velvet trousers hung from the curtain rail beside her. I went to her and we sat on the stairs and looked at them. This time, like her, I felt scared.

The conversation did not go where it should. Another global phenomenon, but who invented trousers? What gods did the horse riders of China worship? The paleolithic Siberians? Wasn't this simply cultural imperialism?

Government information and advice was, as ever, hopelessly out of tune with ordinary people's lives. "Nothing but trousers to wear? I say! Stay at home ladies! It's time to get the sewing machines out."

But again, there were deaths, ludicrous and sad, and in even greater numbers. A 3,000 car pile-up across the eighteen lanes of Canada's Highway 401. Blinded, confused, and half-suffocated by their instantly altered clothing, drivers lost control of vehicles. The frail and alone struggled and cried for help and fell still. Masie and I lived through sheer luck. We had each other.

Once again the hospitals struggled to function. I became part of a volunteer army that cut and sewed, cut and sewed.

When I'd calmed down and thought about it I could only come to one conclusion: Someone or something, call it what you will, some great entity was having a laugh at our expense. I didn't like it.

Distressed as she was, Masie was more sanguine.

'The universe never made sense anyway, not really. I mean, there are rules like the inverse square law of gravity, but all these muons and baryons and quarks, yes they exist, but the way they all interact doesn't actually make *sense*. None of it ever felt reasonable.'

I didn't know. They were what we had, and at least they explained things. Some things.

'They don't explain anything,' Masie insisted. 'They just are.'

Nothing explained what had just happened. Every bolt and scrap of cloth was now trousers, enormous to minuscule, from the fabric plasters in my first aid box to the world's biggest tent in Khazakhstan, now the world's biggest pair of trousers.

Dark matter forms eighty-five percent of the matter in the universe, great ribbons of it connect galaxies together. Perhaps, scientists hypothesised, the solar system was passing through one of those bands and the laws of cause and effect had somehow changed.

It sounded like desperation to me, wild guesswork. We needed to face up to reality. The problem was, nobody had any idea what that meant any more. If this really was reality I wondered how much more we could stand.

Then all the bricks grew wings.

I woke to their gentle rustling hum as they beat on the outside of our home like the slow shifting of some enormous duvet. I stood on the back doorstep and at first thought some strange new vine had grown overnight and covered the walls in delicate beautiful leaves about the same length as my hand, earth tone reds and greens shot with gold, all shifting and shimmering in the breeze. And my neighbour's house, and theirs, all the way down the street. Dressed in a remade t-shirt and crudely reknitted jumper I stood in my small garden where the seedling growth of new grass and weeds and two precious trees were slowly re-greening the brown earth. I could have accepted that new strangeness, but then some phase change passed through them and like the cells of a heart the wings synchronised, beat in rhythm, and I saw them for what they were. It was too much, and temporarily I was undone, unable to accept what I was seeing was real, unable to think in any coherent way.

Masie found me sitting on the bluebell-broken step looking into nowhere. She led me inside and sat me down then sat beside me and pulled my head down into her lap. I don't remember. One moment I was outside, the next, indoors with her and the sun had moved.

Over the next few hours I struggled to put myself back together again. Masie was my rock, my sea-anchor in this strange storm and I needed to be hers.

At the front door I carefully lifted a brick from the drive, worried I might hurt the transmogrified thing, but it was still just a brick, a solid, baked thing, except now it had wings.

As soon as I'd lifted it free the wing pressed to the earth began to beat and I had another odd moment where I fell away from myself, unable to think or function, unable to cope. I wandered back inside and put the brick on the table. Feathered muscle and bone segued seamlessly into each side of the brick. The wings furled briefly, then opened again and began to beat, the steady powerful rhythm of sustained flight.

The bricks were far too heavy for the short if beautiful wings to lift them. And even if they could there were no tail feathers, no mind to guide them. They were bricks.

I couldn't sleep in the house, not knowing that trapped under the plaster and wallpaper were hundreds, possibly thousands of wings all striving to beat. The weather was fine but cold, I carried blankets and pillows outside, all effectively re-purposed woollen and cotton trousers, unpicked and restitched from the trouser apocalypse. It still sounded utterly ridiculous to say it, though that was exactly what it was.

Masie joined me with a thermos of hot water, two mugs and a single precious tea bag, already twice-used. We sat close together with blankets wrapping our knees and shoulders, a huddle of comfort and companionship. Our teas steamed in the cool air, above us, a moonless night sky. Imperceptibly the constellations swung as satellites sped beneath them.

Masie looked down at the newly emerging grass. 'I think we're in a simulation.'

I'd always struggled with the idea. In Newton's era we thought we lived in a clockwork, predictable universe, before that, all things happened because God willed it. It seemed to me the concept was simply of the moment, a function of our own level of technology, philosophy, and understanding. Except over the centuries our understanding had advanced, and in a world, a solar system, possibly an entire universe, where things had stopped making sense perhaps Masie's idea really was the actual explanation. Except...

'I don't feel like a simulation.'

'Me neither, but what do we have to go on? Sample of one.'

'So why do you say so?'

'I think it explains what's going on. It's like how our vision works. Wherever we look we see the fine detail, but the rest of our field of vision is vague, we mostly make it up. It's a simplified approximation and those simplifications can make us see things that aren't there.'

Who hasn't caught things in the corner of their eye, turned, and seen nothing?

'So you think the attention of whoever, whatever–?'

'Perhaps.' Masie gave me a tight humourless smile. 'Perhaps.'

The bricks were bricks, they had no way to feed, no way to move. One by one, then in their masses their wings fell still, drawn in tight against their bodies like those of dead birds. Three days after they first changed, the winged bricks on the walls of my house were disturbed by only an occasional rustle. Then, on the fourth day, nothing.

I wondered what could possibly be next.

The days went by, then the weeks. The world, natural and human, struggled to put itself back together again after what we were now beginning to call The Anomalies. Our scrutiny was everywhere, from the macroscopic to the micro. It seemed everything was back to normal. Could our own intense attention be holding reality together? Masie didn't think so and I realised this was simply my forlorn hope. The ground beneath my feet, underpinning my life, would never feel the same again.

'If their attention has moved on what's to say they won't–?' I snapped my fingers.

'Maybe they will, but that will be different to these focus effects. The old laws still apply. Nothing can propagate faster than the speed of light.' She squeezed my hand and looked away. 'If I'm right and they do turn it all off we won't see it coming, we won't even know.'

Since the Anomalies Masie and I had grown closer together than ever before. Our days were filled with little kindnesses between ourselves. Of all our coffee mugs only one had hearts on it, when we made drinks we both invariably gave it to each other. In many ways we'd never been more content.

It became a persistent thought, the difference between happiness and fulfilment. Happiness it seemed to me was a fleeting thing, contentment was much deeper, more permanent. We took great pleasure in nurturing our garden and the local parklands back to life, in seeing the much diminished natural world begin to thrive again. Flowers bloomed, butterflies flew. Sun and rain, clouds in a blue sky.

I did my best to take comfort in what Masie had told me. *The old laws still applied, nothing can propagate faster than light.* If a wave of nothing, of annihilation, was sweeping towards us right now it would be impossible to know. She would always be in my heart. I realised she was looking at me.

We'd never see it coming.

'What?'

'I love you.'

I took her hand. 'And I–'

D.G.

And into the Tunnel, the Train

AS ED WAKES UP he realises that something has gone. He's not sure what, everything is in the house – his keys and glasses; his secret horde of cash; the kettle; the side door from the kitchen out into the back yard.

The double track of the railway has always been there, across the road, far beyond the long grass and just in front of a distant line of trees. He doesn't remember, but everyone tells him so. It doesn't matter, the trains have never stopped at the town. He wonders which came first, chicken and egg, the town or the track?

The daisies in his front lawn obsess him. Whatever he tries, they remain, a few here, a few there. Apart from the daisies the lawn is perfect, no clover, no moss, every blade green and upright, the edges ruler-straight. By far and away it is the finest front lawn in the street.

Something is missing. Things change, changing all the time. The blue mountains on the southern horizon, the ones he remembers holidaying among with his parents as a child. They had a cabin by one of the myriad blue, pine-fringed lakes and he never understood why they sold it When he was older he went camping with his friends, and later with his own children, Mitch, and Jessica who never visits. Even the mountains don't look the same.

His neighbours try to dissuade him from going there. "It's such a long drive." "You can never go back, Ed, it won't be like you remember." "Wait for Mitch, he'll take you."

He's fixated by the idea and wants to leave straight away. He makes a sandwich, he'd like a BLT but there's no bacon, so cheese and tomato will do. He'd make a flask of tea too but can't find the thermos. Maybe that's what is missing. He starts a new shopping list:

Bacon

Thermos

He's sure there was something else. He can't remember.

Somehow it's late. For a trip to the mountains they'd always start at dawn. He goes anyway and the journey is longer and more stressful than he remembers. He arrives exhausted, caught up in the relentless fast-moving traffic of the highway.

The parking zone is pot-holed and deserted, and the mountains are small, the paths nothing more than a series of ramps winding through bare crags. Up here, along a particular path, he remembers a grand view. He reaches the bend but the sweeping vista of snow-capped peaks, lakes and steep, fir-clad valleys look like scenery flats, and behind the mountains he stands on are monumental arrays of scaffolding. He tells himself they must have become unstable, but he remembers playing there, climbing, and trekking through and beyond them for days. The cry of a buzzard, the start of a deer in the shadowed glen, leaping waterfalls plunging down into babbling boulder-strewn streams, the turn and dip and rise of ferny paths through the pine-scented air.

There's movement on the scaffolding, people, tiny with distance. He follows the sway of buckets on ropes lofting up and down, and hears the clink of hammer on chisel against stone. Stabilisation, he tells himself again, but it's more as if, piece by piece, they are taking the mountains away.

Why do things have to constantly change, can there never be a moment when everything is as it should be? He eats half his sandwich then sits in his car in the empty car park until dusk. Although the journey home is more like the fast open road he remembers, with much lighter traffic, driving into the setting sun, then through the twilight, is not easy. Later, winding through his home-town streets, much of the place appears monochrome, almost bone white.

In the distance, at night he hears the mournful two-tone horns of the trains, and the steady *clack-click, click-clack* of their wheels over the joints of the rails as they come out of the tunnel and head away across the eastern plains.

This bed is comfortable, but too big. Why did he buy such a big bed? Surely a smaller one would be warmer.

In the morning he swears the line is closer.

He spends all day at the window, watching, and counting the trains. More trains, and much longer ones, leave the tunnel, which he can just see from the edge of his bedroom window, than go into it.

The tracks now run parallel with the road at the end of his garden.

"What's going on?"

"Nothing." Everyone says nothing has changed. "Don't you remember?"

And that's exactly the problem, because he's sure he does remember.

The golden yellow hearts of the daisies in the lawn are the only things with any real colour, the rims of the pure white petals tinged with crimson.

"They're pretty," his son, Mitch, says. "Why don't you leave them?"

His back aches, his knees ache, he straightens up as best he can. "I just thought... I had a dream of a home with a perfect lawn. When I was young I thought I'd like to live somewhere like that."

"Dad, there are more important things."

He wasn't sure.

"Dad, there's things we need to talk about."

"I know." He smiles with genuine affection. Mitch still visits and he's so glad every time, it makes his heart lift. "I know, my lad. Come inside and I'll make us some breakfast."

Mitch taps his watch and sighs. Watches have gone the way of phones, now they measure heartbeat, steps, sleep patterns and more. Telling the time has become incidental.

"All right," Mitch says. "Something light."

The train coming out of the tunnel never ends, day and night, night and day, passenger carriages, livestock and freight trucks, and flatbeds all roll steadily past. *Clack-click, click-clack.* He wonders at the sheer power of the engine. The hoot of the horn comes soft and melodic with distance, he's amazed he can still hear it.

At night white light shines from white lampposts onto white roads and empty sidewalks. The sky is dark except for a plain pale moon. He was sure there used to be trees.

His neighbours are packing up and moving out, loading furniture onto the flatbeds as they roll by at not much more than walking pace. Wardrobes and light fittings, the dog, shrubs and paving. Young Mrs Congreve lifts her car up and loads it onto the train along with her children and the swimming pool. He's amazed at her strength.

"Goodbye," he waves.

Mrs Congreve looks flustered, almost guilty, but her children laugh and wave back. "Goodbye, Ed!"

"Come on," she tells them, "Bed time."

"Where are you going?"

"We're not going anywhere. Do you want to come in and sit down? I'll make some tea."

He'd like some tea.

Although everything is packed and gone, somehow it is all still there. And he IS tired. He sits down on a white leather sofa and spreads his arms along the back.

"This is nice, is it new?"

"No, not really. It's a few years old. You've seen it before, remember?"

"Oh, yes," he lies.

White biscuits on a white plate. They taste of sawdust. Nothing *tastes* any more, not like it used to. The tea is good, hot, and sweet. He drinks the tea, and...

He wakes up in his chair at home.

Everything is white, the carpet and furniture, the blank white pictures on the white walls. In a moment of confused fear he wonders if this is even his home? He checks outside and sees the green rectangle of the lawn and is reassured. A few daisies are showing their golden-hearted heads. He doesn't like to use chemicals anymore because of the worms. He read about that somewhere. A healthy lawn needs the worms for drainage and air. It's easy enough to kick over their casts and the rain does the rest.

He spends an hour on his knees with an old spoon, digging up the daisies. It feels like an hour and suddenly he's ravenous but inside, in the kitchen, the cupboards and the tins and packets on the shelves are all white. White print on white labels and he doesn't know which is which. It seems ridiculous that not only did people sell food labelled that way but also that he would have bought it. What he really fancies is some soup, soup with fresh, crusty bread warm from the oven and smothered with melting butter. The desire is so strong he can actually smell it and stands there with his eyes closed. When he opens them the sun has moved. He opens a tin at random and finds some kind of pale mush with lots of little seeds. Is it soup? It's not how he remembers it, but he warms it up and eats it anyway.

Half the street have folded up their houses and loaded them onto the slow train endlessly emerging from the tunnel. *Clack-click, click-clack.* All his neighbours have gone, their vacant lots nothing but white drives and fences, an abandoned football, an ancient white barbeque. Memories of garden parties come like half-remembered dreams.

Something is missing.

He takes a walk to the end of the street and to his pleasure sees his old school, and opposite it on the corner, the church where he sang in the choir at weddings. And there, the garage where he learned his trade. It becomes urgent that he tells someone about this but when he looks around the streets are empty and when he looks back at the school and garage, they seem to be thin and two-dimensional, like stage sets built into the scrub.

There was a road, but when he turns again the road has gone, and rising through him is a dreadful confusion about where he is because school and church and garage are all from his youth and half a continent away, and he doesn't understand why they are here.

All at once he feels lonely and terribly afraid.

He should have put his shoes on.

The twin rail tracks run across a townless, treeless, mountainless white landscape towards the distant tunnel. Some way off, and hard by the track, is his lonely home with its daisy lawn.

Ed knows he can't stay there. Mitch tells him so. He remembers the way to the shops but the roads won't let him go there. The grass needs cutting and the daisies need digging, but someone has hidden the lock to the shed. He wouldn't mind, he has his tools and he could lever the lock plate off its screws, but someone has hidden the tool shed too. He wishes Mitch was here, and in that moment decides that he'll leave the daisies alone, knowing Mitch would be pleased. He picks a few so he can show him and puts them in a small serpentine vase they bought on some holiday.

He wakes in the dark white night and sees an approaching light. He's amazed to see a train rolling not away from, but *towards* the tunnel. *Click-clack, clack-click.*

It is, he realises with absolute certainty, the train he needs to catch.

For a long desperate moment the bed won't let him get up. This old bed, with a will of its own. He makes a supreme effort and stands hunched and gasping on the hand-made rug staring at his thin shins and mottled feet. He dresses hurriedly, the train is close. His shirt is mis-buttoned, there is no time for socks.

There's nothing Ed needs here. Pack it away, give it away, leave it behind. All he wants is his small vase of daisies.

The train rolls past, not too fast and not too slow. Ed takes hold of the handrail and swings up onto the steps at the end of a passenger carriage. He goes through the half-glass door and finding the entire carriage is empty sits by the window, facing towards the engine, holding the small vase of daisies carefully in his lap with both hands.

Although he cannot see forwards, when the train enters the tunnel he knows that even though it may be after miles and miles of darkness, there is the far tunnel mouth and that it shines with a soft light.

After all that rush for the train he's very tired. He closes his eyes and as he does, he remembers. He remembers everything, he remembers what was missing.

He remembers their name, and for the first time in an age he sees their face.

And although he is alone and riding through the darkest part of the tunnel, he knows that up ahead they are waiting.

D.G

Autumn

It was Halloween, when the veils between the worlds are thin. In a suburban garden, an old woman stood looking down at a mound of earth.

It was a very small mound. Just the size to cover a very small cat.

The old woman wiped her face, leaving a mud-smudge under one eye. Her name was Donella, which means dark-haired, although it had been a long time since that was true.

Behind her, there came a faint, silvery sound, a sound most people probably would not have been able to hear. "So, you've come, then," she said. She didn't turn around.

"Well, yes." The voice behind her was light, and soft. It sounded the way bluebells might sound if they rang. "Aren't you going to look at me?"

"So I can see which face you're wearing today?" Donella said, but she turned around, none the less.

The woman – or not – who stood there was moonlight by day, flossy hair and thin shimmering robes, seeming frail and lovely as a piece of antique Venetian glass. Her name was Rosine.

"Oh, look at you," Rosine said. There was something in her voice that was not quite pity, something more like puzzlement.

"If you must," Donella said.

"But you used to be so *lovely,*"

Donella laughed, cracked and crowlike. "Beauty's in the eye of the beholder," she said. "So's ugliness."

"It's soon mended, though," Rosine said, raising her hand.

"I earned this face," Donella said. "Don't you *dare*."

Rosine blinked, and might, actually, have taken a half step backwards, before she laughed. "Oh, now, really. How would you stop me putting a glamour on you? You gave up all your power for...well, *this*." She waved one jewelled and lovely hand at the old woman, the small, suburban house, the small, suburban garden now brown and muddy with autumn, the very small mound of earth.

"Yes. Yes, I did." Donella looked down at her arthritic, age-spotted hands, smeared with damp soil. They had been lovely once, and jewelled, and she had woven wonders with them.

She bent down, and laid one hand briefly on top of the little mound. "Bye-bye, sweetie. Have fun in the next one." Then she straightened, with a grunt. "I made a cake," she said. "If you want some."

"Eat your food? Come now."

"It doesn't work the other way round. You know that as well as I do. I'm going in, and I'm having cake. Come or not, as you want."

Rosine followed Donella in, though she hesitated on the threshold, and stepped over with a shiver that made everything about her flicker, as though she were a transmission from somewhere else.

She wandered around the room, prodding at things, or at least near them, as though actually touching them might stain those long, pale fingers.

Donella washed her hands, and put slices of cake on two plates. It was ginger cake, rich and dark, smelling like spice and childhood.

"Why did you call me?" Rosine said.

"Why did you answer?"

Rosine shrugged. "I was curious." She looked Donella over. "I really didn't think you'd have changed so much."

"It's been more than sixty years."

"Is that all? And now you're regretting your choice." Rosine smiled. "I knew you would. We all did."

"Did you. So what have *you* been up to?" Donella said, picking up a chunk of cake with arthritic care.

"Oh, you've missed so much! The Lord of the Isles cast off his favourite, and was in *such* a gloom that the seas around his demesne turned quite purple, and it rained for a whole year! Or a month, I forget. An inordinately long time, at any rate. His new favourite is Bothis – you probably don't remember him, because he's a desperately dull creature, which is amusing. The fashion for living jewels – do you remember that? Perhaps it was after your time, *so* charming, but it became tedious, and for a while musical garments were the mode."

"Sounds noisy."

Rosine frowned, as nearly as that perfect face would allow. "A little. A few people tried to harmonise, but..."

"But that would mean being part of something, instead of standing out, wouldn't it?"

"There, you see, you still understand."

"I'm old, not senile."

"What does that mean?"

"Some people lose their minds as they age. Forget things. I haven't, yet."

Rosine shuddered. "How awful."

"Yes."

"Being ugly inside and out!"

"If you say so. What else happened while I was here?"

"The Queen turned the whole castle to green glass, but it made everyone inside look sickly, so she turned it back. Oh, she went *without* a favourite, for a while. She said she was bored with them. *Such* an oddity that was, but it didn't last. I suppose she wanted to try something new."

"Hardly that," Donella said. "She went without a favourite at least once before. Had you forgotten? Perhaps she forgot, too. Maybe immortality doesn't protect you from losing your memory after all, eh?"

"Oh, bah, who can remember every little thing? I *do* remember there was a day when there were a hundred rainbows. No-one would admit to doing it. They all faded away."

"That actually sounds new. I should have liked to see that."

"Of course you would. Oh! And the most *delicious* scandal, Merethryn of Calados insulted the Duke of Bethany, and there was a duel, and poor Merethryn was turned to a frog, not even a nice frog, a horrible, yellow, slimy frog. And Bethany *refused* to turn him back. Even when it turned out that the insult hadn't been meant at all, or so Merethryn claimed."

"He could still talk, then, when he was a frog?"

"Oh, constantly. He followed Bethany everywhere, complaining. Bethany turned him back just so he'd stop being such a bore."

"You'd think Bethany would have stopped turning people into amphibians by now. They never learn anything, but then nor does he. What about you? Scandals, great love affairs, court intrigue?"

"Oh, well, of course. I've been *ever* so busy."

"I'm sure. How long did whatsisname...skinny type, pale, dark hair, wore too much black and brooded like a hen – how long did he last?"

Rosine's perfect brows bent again, "Do you mean Aelfric?"

Donella shrugged. "Possibly."

"He was my great love! We wrote each other poems and walked through the woods and danced so beautifully together, and everyone was *so* jealous..."

"Was? So what happened?"

"A tragedy." A single tear, round and perfect as a dewdrop photoshopped onto a rose, slid down Rosine's face.

"Really?" Donella pressed her finger to the last few crumbs of her cake, and ate them.

"We were going to the Queen's Ball, and he..." Rosine hesitated and turned away. When she realised Donella was simply sitting there, and was not going to press her for more, she gave a little sniff of either sorrow or irritation, and said, "He *insisted* on wearing black. To the Queen's Ball! Even for me, he wouldn't do otherwise. Well, what could I do? I had to renounce him. I wept for, oh, so long! My heart was quite broken."

Donella gave, not a sniff, but a snort.

"Why do you make that ugly noise?"

"Tragedy my wrinkled arse. You were bored, he was probably bored, you found an excuse to look for your next amusement."

"He was *not* bored!" Rosine flushed.

"You're all bored. And boring. Why do you think I left?"

"Oh, and your new mortal life is so exciting! Look at you, old and ugly and alone."

"It has been exciting," Donella said. "And dull and hard and annoying and sweet and...I *made* this cake, you understand? With flour and eggs and spices and heat and my hands. Old and ugly as they are. Do you know how good something tastes that you made, with effort instead of magic? The first time I made a cup of tea, myself, with boiling water, it was the best thing I ever tasted. *Ever.* Even though I scalded myself and broke a cup trying. Maybe because of that. Effort sweetens the result."

"Oh, bah, I don't believe you."

"You don't have to."

"Why are you telling me this, anyway?" Rosine said. "You want to come back."

"What gave you that idea?"

"I thought that was why you invited me."

"I thought about it," Donella said. "Sometimes. When things were very hard, and I hurt, and everything was going wrong. But I knew, if I came back...it would all fade, given long enough." She glanced out at the garden. "I'd forget everything, or at least, it would lose its meaning and its colour and taste, the way everything does, there."

"What do you mean, the way everything does?"

"I had a great love, too, you know. A real one."

"What? A mortal?" Rosine shrugged, pettish. "You should know that never ends well."

"Of course it doesn't. But I'm mortal too, now. And here, at least things *end.*"

"What's good about that?"

"You poor silly child," Donella said.

Rosine laughed sharp as a blade. "We're the same age! Or we were. You don't get to call me child just because you've got old, and ugly. I bet your mortal was ugly too. Uglier than my Aelfric, certainly."

But Donella wasn't even looking at her, she was looking past her, with a smile on her face. "He was beautiful to me. I could look at him all day, because he was *dear*. He was kind and sweet and funny – oh, we laughed so much." She glanced at Rosine. "When was the last time you really laughed, with someone instead of *at* them?"

"I don't know what you mean."

"Well, no, you don't, you poor thing." Rosine bristled, but Donella's gaze had gone past her again.

"So what did you do, you and your great love, that was better than I had with Aelfric?" Rosine snapped.

"We tended the garden."

Rosalie looked out of the window and made a face. "It all looks dead."

"It's not dead, you silly creature. It's *autumn*. Mostly it's just asleep. Yes, some things die, and they make the earth richer, and new things grow. That's how it is here. In spring it'll be full of colour again. So we did that, and we had jobs…"

"What's a job?"

"Oh, that'd take far too long. It's a thing you have to do to live, here. And it's often dull and hard but sometimes it's fun. And we went to the pub. We had cats and plants and friends. Actual friends, who got sick, and had babies, and sometimes moved away or died, who cared about our ordinary little lives. And we cared about their ordinary little lives, too."

"Why?"

"Because everything matters when everything might be the last time." Donella looked down at her plate, and her mouth tightened. She took a breath. "Eventually, it was the last time. It hurt...oh, you can't imagine how it hurt. And I thought about coming back, then, but if I did eventually I'd be the only person to remember him, then the memory would get flat and thin, and he'd fade, and in the end he might stop mattering to me. I couldn't bear that. Besides, I couldn't leave the cat."

"And then the cat died, too."

"Yes."

"And did that hurt?"

"Yes."

"And now you want to come back."

"No."

"What?"

"I told you. I don't want everything I had here to fade into the past and be like a picture you look at and you can't even remember who everyone was or why they were smiling. Yes, it hurt. Some things are *meant* to hurt, because it means they *matter*."

Rosine stared at her, with her beautiful ageless eyes that changed colour with her mood, and just now were a pearly, puzzled silver. "But he's *gone*. You'll never see him again."

"You don't know that. And I can feel love, his love, my love, whenever I want. I just have to remember. Can you remember anything about Aelfric apart from his looks and his poor taste in clothes?"

Rosine looked away and waved one hand dismissively. "You probably wouldn't be allowed back, anyway."

"You don't think? Please, they'd love to have me. I'd be the gossip of a year. Or maybe a month or a week. I'd be something new, anyway, for a little while. You could show me off to the whole court, and tell them all stories of my dull little mortal life, and how exciting it would all be. Until it wasn't. Isn't that why you came? To try and persuade me?"

Rosine turned away, hunching one shoulder, and picking her untouched cake to bits. "*You're* the one who made the invitation, not me."

"You're the one who answered."

"Tell me why you invited me, then."

Donella sighed. "We were friends, or something like it." She got to her feet. "If you're not going to eat that cake you can stop making all those crumbs for me to sweep up."

"Tell me!"

"I don't know, all right? Maybe I wanted a reminder of why I made the right decision. Maybe I wanted someone to remember me a little longer."

"Won't all your mortal friends remember you?"

"For a while, but as you say, they're mortal."

"All this, and you didn't even have children," Rosine said.

"Nor did you."

"*I* don't need children to be remembered."

"That's not what they're for," Donella said. "I may not have them, but I know that much. Ah, it's silly, anyway. I matter to you no more than anything else does."

"Things do matter to me!"

"I'm sure they do, as much as they can." Donella leaned over her, and patted one of those smooth white hands, still fidgeting with the slice of cake. "Go home. Maybe you'll remember me, for another sixty years. It's more than a lot of us get."

"And what will you do?"

"I'll tend the garden, and go to the pub. I'll watch sunsets, and talk to cats. And make tea, and cake. And I'll remember love as long as I can. And then I'll go on, to whatever comes after. Something, or nothing. I can live with either." She snort-laughed again. "I'll have to die with one of 'em in any case."

Rosine, finally, took a tiny pinch of cake, and put it in her mouth. "That doesn't sound worth it," she said.

Donella only smiled, and looked out at the garden. Then there was a small, silvery noise, and Rosine was gone. Donella realised she'd taken the rest of the cake.

"I'm not supposed to tell you this, but It's said to be haunted," the estate agent said. "I don't know, some people like that sort of thing." She had got the impression that the couple might be those kind of people.

It was a small, suburban house with a small, suburban garden; but the house had a friendly feel and the garden, though autumn-soggy and a little neglected, was, to a knowing eye, rich with promise for spring.

"Who's it haunted by?"

"Your classic White Lady. A beautiful woman. Appears on Halloween, wanders about looking sorry for herself, disappears again."

"That doesn't sound too bad." The couple grinned at each other. "She doesn't scream, or anything, does she?"

"No. Apparently she likes cake, though – if you leave a bit out for her, the garden does well. That's what the neighbours say, anyway."

"I hope she likes heavy cake," said one.

"She'll like yours," said the other, and they stood, arm in arm, looking at the garden as the brief Autumn day burned away.

G.S.

About Prostate Cancer

Prostate cancer is the most common cancer for men.

In the UK over 52,000 men are diagnosed with this cancer every year.

Over 12,000 will die.

On average, one man in eight will be diagnosed. For black men the risk is significantly higher.

Work continues to develop better ways to detect prostate cancer at an early stage.

If you are over 50 you can ask your GP for a blood test to measure PSA. If the level is high you can have further tests. If not, it will set a baseline value against which later tests can be usefully compared.

Acknowledgements

Nobody does anything on their own. I could not have contributed to this book without many other people.

First and foremost, Gaie. Always, and forever.

If it takes a village to raise a child, it can take a hospital to save a life. Thank you to the staff at the Royal Marsden Sutton, including my medical team, led by Dr Alison Read, including Dr Deep Chakrabarti, Dr Babusha Kalra, Dr Lucy Dunn, Dr Stephen Harland; Dr Liz Bancroft and Dr Ann-Brit Jones; Research Nurses Jenni Parmer & Kate Richards; the nursing staff on West Wing; Dr Yasemin Dandil and the clinical psychology team; the technicians, radiologists and others who operate the CT, Bone, MRI, PET scanners, and radiotherapy machines; the departmental administrators; the staff at Maggie's Centre; the outpatients staff, car park attendants, hospital cleaners, and volunteers.

Thank you to Clinical Exercise Physiologist Emily Curtis, and Chris Cottrell, for years of good advice and motivation with strength and exercise. Likewise, the Nonsuch Parkrun and 5KYW Move against Cancer.

I owe special thanks to Wendy French and Audrey Ardern-Jones for giving me the confidence to write, express myself, and use language in new ways.

To my family: Ashley, Thomas, Hayley, Olivia, Zoe, Mat, Casey, and Alfie. You make it all worthwhile. To my sister, Jay, and cousin Richard & Mindy.

To the dozens and scores of people who have shown me nothing but kindness and support. Some of them are Dev Agarwal, Lincoln Alpern, Jim Anderson, Tiffani Angus, Allen Ashley, Neil Atkinson,

Elizabeth-Jane Baldry, Jacey Bedford, Teika Bellamy, Charlotte Bond, Fay Brooke, Helen Callaghan, Anne Charnock, Annie Czajkowski, Roz Clarke, Nat Coles, Peter Colley, Flic Crowley, Theresa Derwin, Chuck Dreyer, Sarah Ellender, Jaine Fenn, Lex Freeth, Phil Gardner, Chris Van Gorder, Lucia Graves, Terry Grimwood, Lizzie Gwillim, Gavin Hall, Joanne Hall, Chris Harlow, Neil Harmer, Joanne Harris, Chrissey Harrison, Mark Henchy, Steve Higgins, Andrew Hook, Ian Howes, Helen Hutchinson, Nigel Johnson, Howard Andrew Jones, Philip Jones, Trevor Jones, Peter Kelly, Scott Lewis, Pia Long, Guy Martland, Jehangir Mehentee, David Thomas Moore, Mark O'Mahony, Marie O'Reagan, Martin Owton, Sumit Paul-Choudhry, Parkrun, Deb Parsons, Andrew Prentis, Ed Prothero, Georgia Prothero, Rosanne Rabinowitz, Kevin Redfern, Em Ross, Jem Ross, Jenny Rowe, Helen Sansum, Manicks Shankar, Kari Sperring, Vaughan Stanger, Pete Sutton, Christopher Teague, Adrian Tchaikovsky, Luke Thomas, Liz Timms, Sara Townsend, Carole Tyrrell, David Wake, Andrew Wallace, Ian Whates, Andrew White, Annette White, Liz Williams, Neil Williamson.

For anyone I have forgotten to include, the omission is mine. Thank you too, you know who you are.

It's hard to know where this list ends. Does it include the optician at Specsavers, worried about his friend who had just been diagnosed with stage 3 prostate cancer, who wished me luck and put a kindly hand on my shoulder? Yes, it does.

D.G.

About the Authors

David Gullen

Born in South Africa and baptised by King Neptune, David Gullen is an SFF writer and occasional editor, with two novels, one collection, and around 50 short stories published. He has been a judge for the Clarke Awards, and helps run the storied Milford SF Conference.

Despite having been injected with radioactive anti-matter and shot with electron-beam guns, he has failed to develop super-powers.

Find out more at https://davidgullen.com

Gaie Sebold

Fantasy writer and occasional poet, Gaie has published five novels (four under her own name and one under a pseudonym), several short stories and a book of poetry. Her sixth book is forthcoming from Rebellion publishing.

She has worked as a cleaner, secretary, waitress, cashier, stage-tour-manager, editor, and charity administrator. She now mostly writes, grows vegetables and experiments with recipes from around the world.

Her website is www.gaiesebold.com.

Gaie and her husband, David, live in leafy suburbia with a small grey cat.

No Secret

The more I think,
The more I'm sure.
Love is all,
There is no more.

Printed in Great Britain
by Amazon